Reconcilable Differences

Gifts and Challenges of Relationships

George Tan

burg Fortress, Minneapolis

Contents

Introduction 3
Series Introduction 4
1 Challenged to Accept 10
2 Challenged to Adapt 18
3 Challenged to Forgive 24
4 Challenged to Give 31
5 Challenged to Appreciate 38
6 Challenged to Commit 44
Appendix 51
    Group directory 51
    Group commitments 52
    Prayer requests 53
    Prayers 54
    Resources 54
    Response form 55

INTERSECTIONS
Small Group Series

Reconcilable Differences
Gifts and Challenges of Relationships

Developed in cooperation with the Division for Congregational Ministries

George S. Johnson, series introduction
Andrea Lee Schieber, Jeffrey Nelson, and Jill Carroll Lafferty, editors
The Wells Group, series design
Cover: Images copyright © 1998 PhotoDisc, Inc.

Materials identified as *LBW* are from *Lutheran Book of Worship*, copyright 1978.

Scripture quotations are from New Revised Standard Version Bible, copyright 1989 Division of Christian Education of the National Council of the Churches of Christ in the United States of America. Used by permission.

Copyright © 1999 Augsburg Fortress
All rights reserved. May not be reproduced.
ISBN 0-8066-3877-X
Manufactured in U.S.A.

1 2 3 4 5 6 7 8 9 0 1 2 3 4 5 6 7 8 9

Introduction

Troubled relationships

Being in a relationship can be like approaching a porcupine—the closer you get the more vulnerable you become. Even the best of relationships go through troubled waters. Every relationship has its difficult times.

Making new friends is never easy. Being and remaining married and raising a family is never easy. Working together as a team is never easy. The reason for these and other difficulties is that people are different in fundamental and profound ways. As Christians we are called to make relational adjustments so that we may mature in our understanding and living of relationships, for every relationship is a priceless gift from God. Unless we intend to live in isolation from others, we have a sacred mandate to preserve and enhance our relationships: "All this is from God, who reconciled us to himself through Christ, and has given us the ministry of reconciliation" (2 Corinthians 5:18).

Relational adjustments

The purpose of this resource is to help you discover six practical and logical steps to deal with human relationships. As a small group you will be given the opportunity to explore these six interconnected stages toward reconciling differences. You will learn to:

- discover God's design and desire for reconciliation.
- understand the behavioral precept of "give and take" to deal with opposites.
- embrace the reality of forgiveness and forbearance in the face of irreconcilable differences.
- share your gifts and talents with each other.
- explore the importance of self-esteem and the appreciation of others.
- model a long-term relationship after God's long-suffering love.

Healthy relationships

As you begin this resource, realize that nurturing healthy relationships has everything to do with developing love that can last a lifetime—in the family, in the community, in society at large, for oneself, and for others who are different from us. The love of God reconciles us, both to God and to each other. Patience can help you as you practice these six interconnected stages toward nurturing relationships and reconciling differences. We live in an imperfect world and behavioral changes take time. Sometimes it seems as though the world never changes. Patience is our life preserver against despair.

Finally, healthy and reconciled relationships with others depend on a close relationship with God. Time in prayer, worship, and service to God will enable us to realize growth, change, and peace in relationships. Our desire for harmonious living is demonstrated in our freedom to be the people God meant us to be. The more we get a sweet taste of living out our true identities in Christ, the more we will be excited about the prospect of imitating Christ in our interpersonal relationships.

Introducing the series

Welcome into the family of those who are part of small groups! Intersections Small Group Series will help you and other members of your group build relationships and discover ways to connect the Christian faith with your everyday life.

This book is prepared for those who want to make a difference in this world, who want to grow in their Christian faith, as well as for those who are beginning to explore the Christian faith. The information in this introduction to the Intersections small-group experience can help your group make the most out of your time together.

Biblical encouragement

Do not be conformed to this world, but be transformed by the renewing of your minds, so that you may discern what is the will of God—what is good and acceptable and perfect.
Romans 12:2

Small groups provide an atmosphere where the Holy Spirit can transform lives. As you share your life stories and learn together, God's Spirit can work to enlighten and direct you.

Strength is provided to face the pressures to conform to forces and influences that are opposed to what is "good and acceptable and perfect." To "be transformed" is an ongoing experience of God's grace as we take up the cross and follow Jesus. Changed lives happen as we live in community with one another. Small groups encourage such change and growth.

What is a small group?

A number of definitions and descriptions of the small-group ministry experience exist throughout the church. Roberta Hestenes, a Presbyterian pastor and author, defines a small group as an intentional face-to-face gathering of three to twelve people who meet regularly with the common purpose of discovering and growing in the possibilities of the abundant life.

Whatever definition you use, the following characteristics are important.

Small—Seven to ten people is ideal so that everyone can be heard and no one's voice is lost. More than twelve members makes genuine caring difficult.

Intentional—Commitment to the group is a high priority.

Personal—Sharing experiences and insights is more important than mastering content.

Conversational—Leaders that facilitate conversation, rather than teach, are the key to encouraging participation.

Friendly—Having a warm, accepting, nonjudgmental atmosphere is essential.

Christ-centered—The small-group experience is biblically based, related to the real world, and founded on Christ.

Features of Intersections Small Group Series

A small-group model

A number of small-group ministry models exist. Most models include three types of small groups:

- *Discipleship groups*—where people gather to grow in Christian faith and life
- *Support and recovery group*s—where there is a focus on special interests, concerns, or needs
- *Ministry groups*—where there is a task-oriented focus

Intersections Small Group Series offers material for all of these.

For discipleship groups, this series offers a variety of courses with Bible study at the center. What makes a discipleship group different from traditional group Bible studies? In discipleship groups, members bring their life experience to the exploration of the biblical material.

For support and recovery groups, Intersections Small Group Series offers topical material to assist group members in dealing with issues related to their common experience, hurt, or interest. An extra section of facilitator helps in the back of the book will assist leaders of support and recovery groups to anticipate and prepare for special circumstances and needs that may arise as group members explore a topic.

Ministry groups can benefit from an environment that includes prayer, biblical reflection, and relationship building, in addition to their task focus. *Community Builders: 50 Exercises for Church Groups*, from Intersections Small Group Series, helps committees become communities.

Four essentials

Prayer, personal sharing, biblical reflection, and a group ministry task are part of each time you gather. These are all important for Christian community to be experienced. Each of the six chapter themes in each book includes:

- short prayers to open and close your time together.
- carefully worded questions to make personal sharing safe, nonthreatening, and voluntary.
- a biblical base from which to understand and discover the power and grace of God. God's Word is the compass that keeps the group on course.
- a group ministry task to encourage both individuals and the group as a whole to find ways to put faith into action.

Flexibility

Each book contains six chapter themes that may be covered in six sessions or easily extended for groups that meet for a longer period of time. Each chapter theme is organized around two to three main topics with supplemental material to make it easily adaptable to your small group's needs. You need not use all the material. Most themes will work well for 1½- to 2-hour sessions, but a variety of scheduling options is possible.

Bible-based

Each of the six chapter themes in the book includes one or more Bible texts printed in its entirety from the New Revised Standard Version Bible. This makes it easy for all group members to read and learn from the same text. Participants will be encouraged through questions, with exercises, and by other group members to address biblical texts in the context of their own lives.

User-friendly

The material is prepared in such a way that it is easy to follow, practical, and does not require a professional to lead it. Designating one to be the facilitator to guide the group is important, but there is no requirement for this person to be theologically trained or an expert in the course topic. Many times options are given so that no one will feel forced into any set way of responding.

Group goals and process

1. Creating a group covenant or contract for your time together will be important. During your first meeting, discuss these important characteristics of all small groups and decide how your group will handle them.

Confidentiality—Agreeing that sensitive issues that are shared remain in the group.

Regular attendance—Agreeing to make meetings a top priority.

Nonjudgmental behavior—Agreeing to confess one's own shortcomings, if appropriate, not those of others, and not giving advice unless asked for it.

Prayer and support—Being sensitive to one another, listening, becoming a caring community.

Accountability—Being responsible to each other and open to change.

Items in your covenant should be agreed upon by all members. Add to the group covenant as you go along. Space to record key aspects is included in the back of this book. See page 52.

2. Everyone is responsible for the success of the group, but do arrange to have one facilitator who can guide the group process each time you meet.

The facilitator is not a teacher or healer. Teaching, learning, and healing happen from the group experience. The facilitator is more of a shepherd who leads the flock to where they can feed and drink and feel safe.

Remember, an important goal is to experience genuine love and community in a Christ-centered atmosphere. To help make this happen, the facilitator encourages active listening and honest sharing. This person allows the material to facilitate opportunities for self-awareness and interaction with others.

Leadership is shared in a healthy group, but the facilitator is the one designated to set the pace, keep the group focused, and enable the members to support and care for each other.

People need to sense trust and freedom as the group develops; therefore, avoid "shoulds" or "musts" in your group.

3. Taking on a group ministry task can help members of your group balance personal growth with service to others.

In your first session, identify ways your group can offer help to others within the congregation or in your surrounding community. Take time at each meeting to do or arrange for that ministry task. Many times it is in the doing that we discover what we believe or how God is working in our lives.

4. Starting or continuing a personal action plan offers a way to address personal needs that you become aware of in your small-group experience.

For example, you might want to spend more time in conversation with a friend or spouse. Your action plan might state, "I plan to visit with Terry two times before our next small-group meeting."

If you decide to pursue a personal action plan, consider sharing it with your small group. Your group can be helpful in at least three ways: by giving support; helping to define the plan in realistic, measurable ways; and offering a source to whom you can be accountable.

5. Prayer is part of small-group fellowship. There is great power in group prayer, but not everyone feels free to offer spontaneous prayer. That's okay.

Learning to pray aloud takes time and practice. If you feel uncomfortable, start with simple and short prayers. And remember to pray for other members between sessions.

Use page 53 in the back of this book to note prayer requests made by group members.

6. Consider using a journal to help reflect on your experiences and insights between meeting times.

Writing about feelings, ideas, and questions can be one way to express yourself; plus it helps you remember what so often gets lost with time.

The "Daily Walk" component includes material that can get your journaling started. This, of course, is up to you and need not be done on any regular schedule. Even doing it once a week can be time well spent.

How to use this book

The material provided for each session is organized around some key components. If you are the facilitator for your small group, be sure to read this section carefully.

The facilitator's role is to establish a hospitable atmosphere and set a tone that encourages participants to share, reflect, and listen to each other. Some important practical things can help make this happen.

- Whenever possible meet in homes. Be sure to provide clear directions about how to get there.
- Use name tags for several sessions.
- Place the chairs in a circle and close enough for everyone to hear and feel connected.
- Be sure everyone has access to a book; preparation will pay off.
- Have Bibles available and encourage participants to bring their own.

Welcoming

This study deals with complex personal emotions in relational situations. A meeting place that can provide uninterrupted space and time and foster personal and caring conversations, such as a quiet room in the church or a private home, is vital to the learning experience. In order for group members to express their inner feelings openly and honestly, the facilitator needs to stress confidentiality to the group. This study focuses on both topical material and participants' relational struggles.

Always begin and end with prayer. A comfortable seating arrangement is a must and it is always desirable to offer refreshments for relaxation and fellowship.

Focus

Each of the six chapter themes in this book has a brief focus statement. Read it aloud. It will give everyone a sense of the direction for each session and provide some boundaries so that people will not feel lost or frustrated trying to cover everything. The focus also connects the theme to the course topic.

Community building

This opening activity is crucial to a relaxed, friendly atmosphere. It will prepare the ground for gradual group development. Two "Community Building" options are provided under each theme. With the facilitator giving his or her response to the questions first, others are free to follow.

One purpose for this section is to allow everyone to participate as he or she responds to nonthreatening questions. The activity serves as a check-in time when participants are invited to share how things are going or what is new.

Make this time light and fun; remember, humor is a welcome gift. Use fifteen to twenty minutes for this activity in your first few sessions and keep the entire group together.

During your first meeting, encourage group members to write down names and phone numbers (when appropriate) of the other members, so people can keep in touch. Use page 51 for this purpose.

Discovery

This component focuses on exploring the theme for your time together, using material that is read and questions and exercises that encourage sharing of personal insights and experiences.

Reading material includes a Bible text with supplemental passages and commentary written by the topic writer. Have volunteers read the Bible texts aloud. The main passage to be used is printed so that everyone operates from a common translation and sees the text.

"A Further Look" is included in some places to give you additional study material if time permits. Use it to explore related passages, material, or questions.

Questions and exercises related to the theme will invite personal sharing and storytelling. Keep in mind that as you listen to each other's stories, you are inspired to live more fully in the grace and will of God. Such exchanges make Christianity relevant and transformation more likely to happen. Caring relationships are key to clarifying one's beliefs. Sharing personal experiences and insights is what makes the small group spiritually satisfying.

Most people are open to sharing their life stories, especially if they're given permission to do so and they know someone will actively listen. Starting with the facilitator's response usually works best. On some occasions you may want to break the group into units of three or four persons to explore certain questions. When you reconvene, relate your experience to the whole group. If your group includes couples, encourage them to separate for this smaller group activity. Appoint someone to start the discussion.

Wrap-up

Plan your schedule so that there will be enough time for wrapping up. This time can include work on your group ministry task, review of key discoveries during your time together, identifying personal and prayer concerns, closing prayers, and the Lord's Prayer.

The facilitator can help the group identify and plan its ministry task. Introduce the idea and decide on your group ministry task in the first session. Tasks need not be grandiose. Activities might include:

- ministry in your community, such as adopting a food shelf, clothes closet, or homeless shelter; sponsoring equipment, food, or clothing drives; or sending members to staff the shelter.

- ministry to members of the congregation, such as writing notes to those who are ill or bereaved.

- congregational tasks where volunteers are always needed, such as serving refreshments during the fellowship time after worship, stuffing envelopes for a church mailing, or taking responsibility for altar preparations for one month.

Depending upon the task, you can use part of each meeting time to carry out or plan the task.

In the "Wrap-up," allow time for people to share insights and encouragement and to voice special prayer requests. Just to mention someone who needs prayer is a form of prayer. The "Wrap-up" time may include a brief worship experience with candles, prayers, and singing. You might form a circle and hold hands. Silence can be effective. If you use the Lord's Prayer in your group, select the version that is known in your setting. There is space on page 54 to record the version your group uses. Another closing prayer is also printed on page 54. Before you go, ask members to pray for one another during the week. Remember also any special concerns or prayer requests.

Daily walk

Seven Bible readings and a verse, thought, and prayer for the journey related to the material just discussed are provided for those who want to keep the theme before them between sessions. These brief readings may be used for devotional time. Some group members may want to memorize selected passages. The Bible readings also can be used for supplemental study by the group if needed. Prayer for other group members also can be part of this time of personal reflection.

A word of encouragement

No material is ever complete or perfect for every situation or group. Creativity and imagination will be important gifts for the facilitator to bring to each theme. Keep in mind that it is in community that we are challenged to grow in Jesus Christ. Together we become what we could not become alone. It is God's plan that it be so.

For additional resources and ideas see *Starting Small Groups—and Keeping Them Going* (Minneapolis: Augsburg Fortress, 1995).

1 Challenged to Accept

Focus

It is God's design and desire that we work toward harmonious unity in our complex diversity. Acceptance of each other is the first step in reconciling differences.

Community building

The facilitator should begin.

Option

In light of the following situations, respond to this question: "How many extra-strength pain relievers do I need for this? None? Two? A whole bottle?" Briefly explain the reason for your answer.

a. an argumentative person responding to task instructions
b. a micromanager in the workplace
c. an unfaithful spouse confessing a misdeed
d. a disagreeable neighbor with a barking dog
e. a "never on time" person
f. a long-winded preacher

- Say your name and the reason for your interest in this topic.
- Name an image that represents your experience of each of the following environments and share the reason for your image. (For example, "The workplace is like a dagger. Everyone is trying to stab each other in the back.")
    a. home environment
    b. work/school environment
    c. social life environment
    d. church environment
    e. other

Opening prayer

Help us, O God, to bring our weaknesses to your strength. In your love, teach us to be open to the people we cannot accept and help us to grow beyond the people we are. Amen

Discovery

Read aloud and discuss the questions that follow.

2 Corinthians 5:17-20

17 So if anyone is in Christ, there is a new creation: everything old has passed away; see, everything has become new! 18 All this is from God, who reconciled us to himself through Christ, and has given us the ministry of reconciliation; 19 that is, in Christ God was reconciling the world to himself, not counting their trespasses against them, and entrusting the message of reconciliation to us. 20 So we are ambassadors for Christ, since God is making his appeal through us; we entreat you on behalf of Christ, be reconciled to God.

- What is a person who has been reconciled to Christ like?
- What does *reconcile* mean to you?
- What are some costs of the ministry of reconciliation?

What is reconciliation?

Read aloud.

The essence of reconciliation is that our lives are changed in Christ when we experience the healing of a relationship. Since our reconciliation with God is intimately tied to our reconciliation with each other, this new life in Christ, empowered by the Holy Spirit, enables us to look at all of our interpersonal relationships in new ways. Certainly we cannot claim peace with God unless we are at peace with our neighbors. Thus, the "old has passed away . . . everything has become new" (2 Corinthians 5:17). As Christians reconciled in Christ, the Holy Spirit sets us free to see everyone differently, full of bold and beautiful possibilities. When the effects of this Christ-reconciled life move into the home, the workplace, the church, and the community, we will learn to accept people as we begin to heal struggling relationships.

Lead the group in this exercise.

■ Complete the following sentences to reflect what reconciling differences could mean to you.

a. Being made new means that I can _____.

b. When I am reconciled to God, I _____.

c. Given this ministry of reconciliation, I am called to _____.

d. Becoming an ambassador for Christ means I _____.

e. The best thing about my reconciled relationship with God is _____.

Discovery

A letter from Sam

Read aloud and discuss the questions that follow.

Hello. I am Sam and I have AIDS. If you had known I have AIDS, you probably would have avoided any contact with me even though I don't show any physical signs of the disease. But that's okay because I am used to it.

Many people have contracted the disease in many ways. But all of us have become outcasts in some sense. I'll tell you one thing: I'd rather live with any other disease than live with AIDS and be treated like a social outcast.

I am scared! My life has been threatened and my property vandalized. People call me names and shake their fingers at me. Doesn't anybody know how I hurt inside? I need people to care for me and accept me. Do you have any idea what it's like to have no friends? Maybe I should just go ahead and kill myself! After all, others certainly have killed me with their fear and hatred. Sometimes I even think God doesn't accept me anymore; the way "Christians" treat me tells me that.

I don't know what I want. Some simple human sympathy from the people around me? A smile from a distance? I know I would like to have someone believe in me and accept me. Would you be willing to be my friend? Please!

Signed,

Sam, the outcast!

- What would be difficult about accepting Sam as your neighbor?

- How do our social norms, personal biases, and spiritual upbringing come into play in this story?

- What do you think the people of Jesus' time did when they saw him touching someone with leprosy or associating with tax collectors and prostitutes?

A further look

Read aloud. Then ask a volunteer to read Acts 10:1-35.

Seeking unity in our relationships is like running an obstacle course. We need to hurdle our own cultural upbringings, social norms, personal habits, and learned prejudices in order to open our lives to enjoy the people who are different from us. Acts 10 challenges us to examine our own prejudices toward the "unclean" in our midst and realize that in Christ, God can make the unclean holy. In this passage we can see a unique interaction between Cornelius, a Gentile Roman, and the apostle Peter, a circumcised Jew who is living with Simon the tanner, a Christian engaged in a profession deemed unclean.

- Who are the "unclean" and the "holy" in your home, work, or worship environment?

- With whom do you have difficulty? How are you different? How are you alike?

- What barriers do you need to remove before you can reconcile with each other?

- What do you need to change in order to accept diversity in unity?

Discuss.

Consider this

"Where all think alike, none thinks very much."

"Lutheran Brotherhood's Newsletter Nuggets" vol. 2, no.3

■ Share a time when someone who is different from you challenged you to change your thinking, your speaking, or your routine. How did it feel at the time? How does it feel now?

Discovery

The Babel conspiracy

Read or ask a group member to read aloud Genesis 11:1-9.

The story of the Tower of Babel is not so much about human pride as human fear. In light of God's purpose for humanity to be "scattered" (Genesis 11:4b, 8-9), to become people of many nations and cultures, humanity tried to create an artificial unity of self-sufficiency and autonomy called the Tower of Babel. To be scattered over the face of the earth was not an act of punishment by God, but an act of blessing. God willed multiethnicity, and like our God who is three-in-one, humanity is also meant to be divisible, yet one. We are divided by culture, language, social behavior, and personal habits, yet we are united in our loyalty and worship of God.

■ Is diversity the plan or punishment of God?

■ What are the fears that keep us separate from those who are different from us?

- Share examples of how we impose artificial unity upon others to create homogeneity in the home, workplace, church, and community?

- How can we assert our own cultural uniqueness or personal preferences without slighting others who are different?

Discuss as a group.

Consider this

Japanese Buddha | Taoist symbol | Ganesha (Hindu)

Star of David | Egyptian Ankh | Moon and Star

- Share with the group an experience of being in a different religious environment. What were your thoughts? Your feelings? Your insights?

Pull it together

Complete this exercise individually. Notes can be recorded on page 52 under "Personal Action Plan."

- Complete the following survey to measure your own relationship skills. Rate each statement on a scale of 1 to 10 for your present position (1 = never, 5 = some of the time, and 10 = always). Refer to this exercise periodically in order to measure your own improvement as you move through this study process.

    a. I understand people. _____
    b. I know how to deal with difficult people. _____
    c. I can adjust in my relationships. _____
    d. I feel good about myself. _____

e. I can forgive and forget. _____
f. I am generous with others. _____
g. I appreciate the people around me. _____
h. Others find me likeable. _____
i. I feel close to God. _____
j. I love my family. _____
k. I like my colleagues. _____
l. I get along with my neighbors. _____
m. I feel close to my church family. _____
n. I am adaptable to change. _____

Group goals

Invite the group to agree on goals and commitments for their time together, and record under "Group Commitments" on page 52.

As you study this resource, where do you want to journey together as a group? Consider the following suggestions for group goals or write your own. Choose at least two group goals.

a. Help each other identify at-risk relationships so that each person can begin to plan and implement the work of reconciliation.
b. Begin a journal to record the process of reconciling those relational differences and use this journal for group support and sharing.
c. Complete this resource together and help each other gain a new perspective on reconciling differences.
d. Encourage group members to appreciate the people in their lives.
e. Create an intimate caring unit throughout the study of this series.

Group commitments

As you journey together, what can you do for each other along the way? Use the following suggestions or create your own list that will enhance individual learning. See the series introduction (page 4) for information.

a. Pray for each other to find strength and determination to resolve relational differences.
b. Encourage and provide emotional support for each other beyond the small-group meeting.
c. Maintain confidentiality in the group.
d. Set a high priority for regular attendance for the group meetings.
e. Begin and end on time.

Wrap-up

See page 9 in the introduction for a description of "Wrap-up."

Before you go, take time for the following:

- Group ministry task

- Review

See page 54 for suggested closing prayers. Page 53 can also be used for listing ongoing prayer requests.

- Personal concerns and prayer concerns

- Closing prayers

Daily walk

Bible readings

Day 1
Psalm 133:1-3

Day 2
John 13:34-35

Day 3
Romans 12:15-18

Day 4
Ephesians 4:4-6

Day 5
1 Peter 3:8-10

Day 6
Ezekiel 37:17-23

Day 7
Hebrews 10:19-25

Verse for the journey

"Salt is good; but if salt has lost its saltiness, how can you season it? Have salt in yourselves, and be at peace with one another" (Mark 9:50).

Thought for the journey

A common misinterpretation of the Western democratic concept of equality is to confuse it with uniformity. What do you think about this misinterpretation? What practical steps can you take this week to embrace equality in diversity?

Prayer for the journey

Help us, O God, that our pride not bear the fruit of conceit, and that our thoughtlessness not destroy others. Show us that our realization of your design and desire for harmonious unity will allow us to accept each other as you accept us. Amen

2 Challenged to Adapt

Focus

When we change our perception of others through a creative and fearless readjustment of personal viewpoints, we honor God and strengthen our resolve to reconcile differences.

Community building

Option

Appearances can be deceiving. Share a time when your opinion about someone dramatically changed because you got to know the person.

■ Read the following statements and discuss the questions.

   a. Welfare recipients are lazy.
   b. Asians are money-grabbers.
   c. Single people are incomplete.
   d. Lawyers are ambulance-chasers.
   e. Rich people are uncaring.
   f. Young people are self-centered.
   g. Management is only concerned about profit margins.

■ What is your reaction to these statements?

■ Why do people make such statements?

Check-in

Share an incident that happened to you since the last meeting, in which you opened yourself to another who was different from you.

■ What did you learn about them? Yourself?

■ How did they react to you?

Opening prayer

Dear God, help us to act toward others as we would wish them to act toward us. May justice and love inspire us to break down all self-centeredness and prejudice. Amen

Discovery

Self-examination

Read aloud.

A Chinese proverb says, "In order to know others we need to know ourselves." Self-awareness and self-acceptance ground us so that we are able to adapt to and accept others who are different from us. In the following passage, Jesus taught that judging others apart from self-reflection and self-criticism hinders relationships by fostering preconceptions and misinformation. To truly appreciate others in their diversity, we first need to examine ourselves.

Matthew 7:3-5

3 Why do you see the speck in your neighbor's eye, but do not notice the log in your own eye? 4 Or how can you say to your neighbor, "Let me take the speck out of your eye," while the log is in your own eye? 5 You hypocrite, first take the log out of your own eye, and then you will see clearly to take the speck out of your neighbor's eye.

Discuss.

- Are you primarily self-critical or critical of others? Explain.
- What do you believe and assume about dealing with people on a daily basis?
- If you are able, share your strengths and weaknesses in interpersonal relationships.

A further look

Cut out photographs of obscure people from magazines and newspapers. Ask the group to describe each person according to the provided list of opposites. Then reveal the identity of each person and ask the questions that follow.

Discuss with a partner.

- Is each person
    a. rich or poor?
    b. educated or uneducated?
    c. successful or unsuccessful?
    d. law-abiding or criminal?
    e. self-giving or self-centered?

- What was the rationale for your choices?

- Are you surprised by the identities of these people? Why or why not?

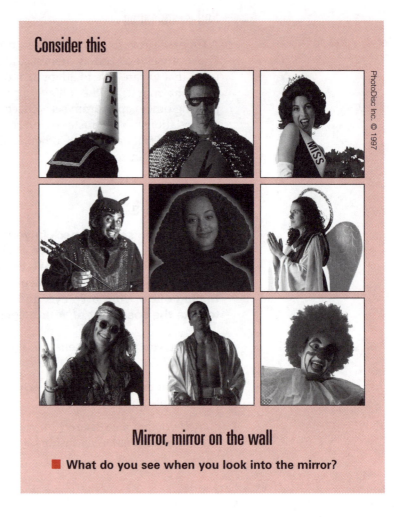

Consider this

Mirror, mirror on the wall

- What do you see when you look into the mirror?

Discovery

Read and complete the exercise.

Power distance

"The perception of personal power is our own understanding of our ability to change our environment. In terms of interpersonal relationships, the perception of power is our sense of authority and ability to influence and control others. More often than not, this perception of power is unconscious. It is part of the 'instinctual' culture." (Eric H. F. Law, *The Wolf Shall Dwell with the Lamb* [St. Louis: Chalice Press, 1993], 14-15.)

Eric Law applies Geert Hofstede's concept of "power distance" in his book, *The Wolf Shall Dwell with the Lamb*. The concept asserts two culture types: "High Power Distance" and "Low Power Distance." In a High Power Distance culture, people accept a hierarchical system of inequality in which a powerless majority is ruled by a powerful elite. In this culture type, everyone has a designated place in society—to rule or to be ruled. In a Low Power Distance culture, by contrast, inequality is minimized. In fact, the power of the people is a basic premise of a democratic society and a hierarchical system exists only for the sake of organizational convenience. China and India, for example, are High Power Distance cultures, and the United States and Germany are Low Power Distance cultures.

- Apply the concept of "power distance" to interpersonal relationships. What is the significance of understanding this concept as found in:

    a. an interracial marriage between a Low Power Distance husband and a High Power Distance wife?
    b. an HPD pastor and an LPD church council?
    c. an HPD parent and LPD children?
    d. an LPD worker and an HPD supervisor?
    e. an HPD mother- or father-in-law and an LPD son- or daughter-in-law?

- Share whether you are an HPD or an LPD person. Explain your conclusion.

- How does your power distance type affect your daily interaction with people?

A further look

Read this prayer and lead a discussion of the questions that follow.

I see white and black, Lord.
I see white teeth in a black face.
I see black eyes in a white face.
Help us to see *persons*, Jesus—not a black person or a white person, a red person or a yellow person, but human persons.

Malcolm Boyd (b. 1923)
American Episcopal priest
<small>*Are You Running with Me Jesus?* by Malcolm Boyd.
Copyright © Malcolm Boyd. Used by permission.</small>

- Can you say "Amen" to this prayer? Explain.

- In what ways has the media shaped your cultural and ethnic tolerance or lack of tolerance?

- Where and with whom can you freely express your feelings about multiethnic tensions?

Consider this

Ask the group to respond to the statement in light of the Bible passages.

To God I am _____

because _____.

   a. Genesis 1:26-27
   b. Psalm 8:3-8
   c. Jeremiah 1:5
   d. Matthew 10:29-31
   e. 1 Corinthians 6:19-20

Pull it together

Provide each group member with a blank piece of paper and a pencil.

- List the problems, as you understand them, in a relationship in which you are struggling.

   a. Circle the problems to which you contribute in this relationship.
   b. Ask the group to offer suggestions for help in this relationship.
   c. Check at least one conciliatory gesture that you will do this week to address the problems in the relationship.
   d. Share this decision with the group.
   e. End with a brief prayer for the person on your left.

Wrap-up

Before you go, take time for the following:

- Group ministry task

- Review

- Personal concerns and prayer concerns

- Closing prayers

Daily walk

Bible readings

Day 1
Psalm 139:1-3,6

Day 2
Galatians 4:7

Day 3
Psalm 139:13-16

Day 4
Proverbs 14:20-21

Day 5
1 Samuel 16:7

Day 6
1 Timothy 4:12

Day 7
1 Timothy 5:1

Verse for the journey

"Take care that you do not despise one of these little ones; for, I tell you, in heaven their angels continually see the face of my Father in heaven" (Matthew 18:10).

Thought for the journey

We are all potential agents of change. If we bring discipline to our learning and adapt new ways, we will experience change in ourselves and bring change to the people around us. What do you think about this statement? What aspects of yourself need to be reexamined to better engage in the task of reconciling differences?

Prayer for the journey

O God, our life reaches out in ever-widening circles. Bless us in the journey and mold us by your Spirit to grow in our understanding and acceptance of others. Amen

ST. ALBAN'S CHURCH
486 RATHGAR AVENUE
WINNIPEG, MANITOBA
R3L 1G3

3 Challenged to Forgive

Focus

When we receive mercy and forgiveness from God, we become children of grace and charity with each other.

Community building

Option

Share one of the following life experiences:

a. a time you felt embarrassed

b. a time you knew grace was given to you

c. a time you found it difficult to apologize

■ Indicate your ease at forgiveness by assigning a number for each of the following life situations (1 = very easy to forgive; 2 = somewhat easy to forgive; 3 = somewhat difficult to forgive; 4 = always difficult to forgive). Briefly explain your choice. How easy is it for you to forgive:

a. a server who spilled a beverage on your new clothes? _____
b. a person who forgot to pass on an important phone message to you? _____
c. the supervisor who put you down in front of the team? _____
d. the pastor for breaking a confidence in a prayer meeting? _____
e. a stranger who honked at you to move through an intersection just after the light turned green? _____
f. yourself for causing pain to someone you truly love? _____
g. your partner for embarrassing you in front of the family? _____

Check-in

■ Share the results of the activity from the "Pull It Together" section of the last session.

■ Offer follow-up suggestions for further action toward reconciliation.

> **Opening prayer**
>
> Merciful Father, release us from our bondage to anger and disappointment so that we may be free to offer peace and hope to others. Amen

Discovery

Romans 8:1-6

Read aloud and discuss.

¹ There is therefore now no condemnation for those who are in Christ Jesus. ² For the law of the Spirit of life in Christ Jesus has set you free from the law of sin and of death. ³ For God has done what the law, weakened by the flesh, could not do: by sending his own Son in the likeness of sinful flesh, and to deal with sin, he condemned sin in the flesh, ⁴ so that the just requirement of the law might be fulfilled in us, who walk not according to the flesh but according to the Spirit. ⁵ For those who live according to the flesh set their minds on the things of the flesh, but those who live according to the Spirit set their minds on the things of the Spirit. ⁶ To set the mind on the flesh is death, but to set the mind on the Spirit is life and peace.

In Christ we have tremendous potential to like the unlikable and imagine the unimaginable. The apostle Paul tells us that spiritual health begins with the way we think and believe at home, at school, in church, and at work. Paul further tells us that God's grace brings about a transformation of the mind that enables us to take new and different approaches to difficulties in life and conduct our interpersonal relationships according to the Spirit rather than the desires of the flesh.

- What does it mean for you to be "in Christ" at home, at school, in church, or at work?
- How do you share grace as it is received?
- What do interpersonal relationships look like when you are transformed in the Spirit rather than conformed to the world?

From disgraced to graced

Invite the group to participate in this dramatic reading. Moving clockwise, individual group members should read the parts labeled "Accused" while the facilitator reads the parts of the "Accuser" and "Jesus." All group members should read the "Satan" part in unison. Make sure the movement in the reading is explained before the group begins.

Accuser: The facts are known: You cheated in your work.

Accused #1: I admit that I did it. I miscalculated the cost and never thought I would be caught.

Satan: Out of this place! You're a disgrace!

Accused #1 leaves the group and stands in a corner.

Accuser: The facts are known: You lied to your spouse.

Accused #2: I admit that I did it. I was fearful that the truth would destroy our love.

Satan: Out of this place! You're a disgrace!

Accused #2 leaves the group and stands in a corner.

Accuser: The facts are known: You schemed and took revenge.

Accused #3: I admit that I did it. I was so angry I couldn't hold back my hate.

Satan: Out of this place! You're a disgrace!

Accused #3 leaves the group and stands in a corner.

Accuser: The facts are known: You stole from the Lord.

Accused #4: I admit that I did it. God is not a priority in my life.

Satan: Out of this place! You're a disgrace!

Accused #4 leaves the group and stands in a corner.

Accuser: The facts are known: You spread hearsay and gossip.

Accused #5: I admit that I did it. I want to control my tongue but I can't.

Satan: Out of this place! You're a disgrace!

Accused #5 leaves the group and stands in a corner.

Allow a moment of silence for reflection on the reading, then begin again.

Jesus: These are my people. I died for them all! Don't point your accusing finger and condemn them to fall.
(To Accused #1) I know you cheated but I saved you on the cross. You are mine forever! *(Accused #1 returns to the group.)*
(To Accused #2) I know you lied but I saved you on the cross. You are mine forever! *(Accused #2 returns to the group.)*
(To Accused #3) I know you hated but I saved you on the cross. You are mine forever! *(Accused #3 returns to the group.)*
(To Accused #4) I know you stole from me but I saved you on the cross. You are mine forever! *(Accused #4 returns to the group.)*
(To Accused #5) I know you spread untruths but I saved you on the cross. You are mine forever! *(Accused #5 returns to the group.)*

All: We are forgiven! Thanks be to God!

- What were your emotions as the group shouted, "Out of this place! You're a disgrace!" and you left the group?
- What were your emotions when you returned? Did you sense God's grace? Why or why not?
- What does it feel like to shout, "Out of this place! You're a disgrace"?
- Do you most identify with the Accuser, the Accused, Satan, or Jesus? Briefly explain your answer.

Read and discuss.

Consider this

"I believe any person who asks for forgiveness has to be prepared to give it."—President William Jefferson Clinton, speaking in the Rose Garden after being acquitted by the U.S. Senate of perjury and obstruction of justice charges

- Do you agree or disagree? Explain.
- What makes it so hard for us to forgive each other in the family? In the workplace? In the church? In society?

Discovery

2 Corinthians 2:5-11

Read aloud and discuss.

5 But if anyone has caused pain, he has caused it not to me, but to some extent—not to exaggerate it—to all of you. 6 This punishment by the majority is enough for such a person; 7 so now instead you should forgive and console him, so that he may not be overwhelmed by excessive sorrow. 8 So I urge you to reaffirm your love for him. 9 I wrote for this reason: to test you and to know whether you are obedient in everything. 10 Anyone whom you forgive, I also forgive. What I have forgiven, if I have forgiven anything, has been for your sake in the presence of Christ. 11 And we do this so that we may not be outwitted by Satan; for we are not ignorant of his designs.

Recall the slogan United We Stand, Divided We Fall. What unites and what divides us? According to Paul, forgiveness is the glue of our unity. If Christians fail to practice forgiveness in their interpersonal relationships, they weaken their witness to Christ in the world. They also weaken the church in its outreach to the world. Think about dysfunctional families, disruptive special interest groups, and divided churches. Our inability to forgive for the sake of unity gives Satan a victory. Paul invites us to practice forgiveness in our relationships for the sake of healing and growth.

- As you stand in the shadow of the cross, what do you find difficult to forgive in your family? In your church family?
- What stands in the way of your practice of forgiveness?
- What is the relationship between forgiveness and unity?
- How does Satan destroy unity through unforgiving attitudes?

A further look

Read this story and discuss.

Once a woman came to her pastor claiming that she spoke with the Lord. Not believing her, the pastor jokingly requested, "Well, Sarah, next time you speak with the Almighty, ask what sins I confessed this morning."

A few days later, the woman returned and the pastor inquired about her latest conversation with the Lord. "Pastor," the woman said, "I did ask the Lord about your confession."

"And what did God tell you?" asked the pastor.

"The Lord said, 'I certainly remember the confession but I have already forgotten the sins!'"

- Why is it so difficult for us as a forgiven people to forgive each other?
- What one thing would you like to improve in your practice of forgiveness? How will you do this?

Discuss as a group.

Consider this

"Our temper gets us into trouble and our pride keeps us there."

"Lutheran Brotherhood's Newsletter Nuggets" vol. 2, no. 4

■ Been there? Done that? Explain.

Pull it together

A Poison Tree

Read aloud and discuss.

I was angry with my friend,
I told my wrath, my wrath did end.
I was angry with my foe:
I told it not, my wrath did grow:

And I water'd it in fears,
Night & morning with my tears;
And I sunned it with smiles,
And with soft deceitful wiles.

And it grew both day and night,
Till it bore an apple bright,
And my foe beheld it shine,
And he knew that it was mine,

And into my garden stole,
When the night had veil'd the pole:
In the morning glad I see
My foe outstretch'd beneath the tree.

William Blake, 1757–1827

■ According to Blake, what happens when one delays forgiveness in a relationship? Do you agree or disagree with Blake? Why or why not?

■ What can you do to initiate peace in a relationship?

Wrap-up

Before you go, take time for the following:

- Group ministry task

- Review

- Personal concerns and prayer concerns

- Closing prayers

Daily walk

Bible readings

Day 1
Daniel 9:18

Day 2
Matthew 5:7

Day 3
Psalm 103:8-10

Day 4
Micah 6:8

Day 5
Matthew 18:33

Day 6
Romans 4:7

Day 7
Matthew 5:44

Verse for the journey

"And if the same person sins against you seven times a day, and turns back to you seven times and says, 'I repent,' you must forgive" (Luke 17:4).

Thought for the journey

Forgiveness is not based on the extent of the sin, but the extent of the forgiver's grace and mercy. What do you think about this statement? What do you need to do to practice forgiveness this week?

Prayer for the journey

O God, if we have failed each other, forgive us. If we have disgraced ourselves, forgive us. If we have grieved you, forgive us. Amen

4 Challenged to Give

Focus

God is the creator of diversity, whose purpose it is to entrust natural abilities and spiritual gifts to all so that we may serve each other as an interdependent people.

Community building

Option

Read this statement and discuss the questions: "None of us has all the gifts. Yet all of us have some of the gifts." Do you agree with this statement? Explain. Give examples to illustrate this statement.

■ Compare yourself to the various people integral to the success of your favorite sports team. Who best describes your usual pattern of behavior in a relationship? Explain your choice(s). In a relationship, I am usually the:

- a. owner of the franchise.
- b. coach.
- c. captain of the team.
- d. mascot.
- e. most valuable player.
- f. cheerleader.
- g. water carrier.
- h. fan in the stands.
- i. referee.
- j. media commentator.

Check-in

■ Share your practice of forgiveness in the past week, both as giver and receiver.

■ Offer suggestions for further action toward reconciliation.

Opening prayer

Help us, O God, as we seek to reconcile differences with the people around us this day, that we may act in your strength, share in your love, and give in your Spirit. Amen

Discovery

Read and discuss.

Matthew 25:14-20, 22, 24-27

14 For it is as if a man, going on a journey, summoned his slaves and entrusted his property to them; **15** to one he gave five talents, to another two, to another one, to each according to his ability. Then he went away. **16** The one who had received the five talents went off at once and traded with them, and made five more talents. **17** In the same way, the one who had the two talents made two more talents. **18** But the one who had received the one talent went off and dug a hole in the ground and hid his master's money. **19** After a long time the master of those slaves came and settled accounts with them. **20** Then the one who had received the five talents came forward, bringing five more talents, saying, "Master, you handed over to me five talents; see, I have made five more talents." . . . **22** And the one with the two talents also came forward, saying, "Master, you handed over to me two talents; see, I have made two more talents." . . . **24** Then the one who had received the one talent also came forward, saying, "Master, I knew that you were a harsh man, reaping where you did not sow, and gathering where you did not scatter seed; **25** so I was afraid, and I went and hid your talent in the ground. Here you have what is yours." **26** But his master replied, "You wicked and lazy slave! . . . **27** you ought to have invested my money with the bankers, and on my return I would have received what was my own with interest."

Together as friends, colleagues, couples, families, or a church, we have a call to share our gifts with one another. The use of the talents in this parable is not as much for self-interest and security as for service to others in the community.

- Do you know your natural gifts? Tell the group about them.

- How can you enrich those around you with your gifts and talents?

- What gifts do you lack that someone else can supply?

A further look

In a culture that prizes individuality and self-sufficiency, often people do not like to admit that they lack certain gifts or abilities and refuse help or guidance from others who may possess these very gifts or abilities. As a result, people become increasingly separated and isolated from one another and do not learn how to live in supportive community. It is no wonder that our differences become a cause for tension rather than celebration.

- Do you lack certain gifts or abilities you wish you possessed? What are they?

- Do you accept help from others who may possess these gifts or abilities? How does the offer of help or your acceptance of help make you feel?

- What would it take for you to be more accepting of the gifts and abilities of others?

Read 1 Corinthians 12:14-27.

- What does Paul say about the diversity of gifts in the community? If Paul's words were taken seriously, what would such a community be like? How would your attitude about your perceived lack of gifts or abilities change?

- What do you think Paul meant in his discussion about "respectable" and "less respectable" members of the body?

- Who are the "respectable" and "less respectable" members of your family? Your community? Your faith community? Why are they considered as such?

- How would Paul's teaching about the body alter the way others are viewed? How would Paul's teaching about the body help reconcile differences between people?

Discuss with a partner.

Consider this

"My personhood includes my personal history, my life situation, and my past and present struggles. No one else can give precisely what I do, because, in giving me a gift, God has called me to use my unique personhood in the passing on of that gift to others."

Gary L. Harbaugh, *God's Gifted People: Discovering Your Personality as a Gift*, expanded ed. (Minneapolis: Augsburg Fortress, 1990), 17

- When you look at yourself holistically, including your past, present, and future, what do you think God had in mind for you in this lifetime?

Discovery

Invite a group member to read the passage, then discuss the questions. Conclude this section by reading the summary paragraph.

1 Corinthians 12:7-11

⁷ To each is given the manifestation of the Spirit for the common good. ⁸ To one is given through the Spirit the utterance of wisdom, and to another the utterance of knowledge according to the same Spirit, ⁹ to another faith by the same Spirit, to another gifts of healing by the one Spirit, ¹⁰ to another the working of miracles, to another prophecy, to another the discernment of spirits, to another various kinds of tongues, to another the interpretation of tongues. ¹¹ All these are activated by one and the same Spirit, who allots to each one individually just as the Spirit chooses.

- What are spiritual gifts and from where do they come?
- What is the purpose of spiritual gifts?
- What is the significance of these gifts in our ability to reconcile differences in the body?
- Imagine what your church would be like if all believers were empowered to serve each other according to their spiritual gifts? Describe that vision to each other.
- Take some time now to affirm the spiritual gifts you see in each other.

The gifts of the Spirit are given to individuals for the sake of ministry in the body of Christ. Not only does this ministry of sharing enhance others, it also makes us aware of our need to receive from others. Such interdependency draws people together for support and encouragement.

A further look

Read aloud and answer the questions as a group.

Once the Carpenter's tools had a meeting. Brother Hammer was asked to leave because he was making too much noise. "If I have to leave then Sister Screwdriver must go, too, because it takes too much effort to turn her around again and again to get her to accomplish anything!"

Sister Screwdriver protested and said, "If I have to leave then Brother Plane must go also because his work is only on the surface without any depth!"

To this Brother Plane complained, "If I have to leave then Sister Rule must go too because she is always measuring as if she were the only one who is accurate around here."

In the middle of the argument, the Carpenter of Nazareth walked in. He went to fashion a boat to be used one day as his pulpit for the word of God. He used the hammer, the screwdriver, the plane, the saw, and the rule. And when it was finished, Sister Saw rose and said, "Dear family, I believe God made us all to be workers together for the Lord."

The Bible talks about the importance of spiritual gifts in the life of the Christian community and lists a number. Here are some.

Apostleship: the gift to start congregations

Prophecy: the gift to proclaim God's truth

Evangelism: the gift to communicate the gospel of salvation

Pastorship: the gift to lead and care for the body of Christ

Teaching: the gift to relate God's word to Christian life

Exhortation: the gift to comfort and encourage the people

Knowledge: the gift to analyze information

Wisdom: the gift to apply knowledge

Help: the gift to enhance others in their ministry

Hospitality: the gift to care for needy people

Giving: the gift to provide resources for God's ministry

Government: the gift to plan and execute God's ministry

Mercy: the gift of support to those who are suffering

Faith: the gift to envision God's will and purpose

Discernment: the gift to decide truth from error

Miracles: the gift to do powerful acts that glorify God

Healing: the gift to restore people to health

Tongues: the gift to speak in spiritual language

Interpretation: the gift to interpret spiritual language

- Which spiritual gifts do you have?
- Are your spiritual gifts recognized and affirmed by this group? Why or why not?
- Are your ministries compatible with your spiritual gifts? Explain.

Consider this

By contrast, the fruit of the Spirit is love, joy, peace, patience, kindness, generosity, faithfulness, gentleness, and self-control. Galatians 5:22-23

■ **What is the difference between spiritual gifts and the fruit of the Spirit?**

Pull it together

■ Create three gift cards to be given away during the next week. For each note card:

    a. Think of someone with whom you can share a gift this week and write his or her name after "To."
    b. Write your name after "From."
    c. Think of a specific thought, action, or personality trait you wish to share.

Be sure to share your gift cards and gifts with each person this week.

Give each group member three 3- by 5-inch note cards. Be sure each card has the words "From Me to You" centered at the top. Down the left margin of each card, print "To," "From," and "My Gift."

Wrap-up

Before you go, take time for the following:

- Group ministry task

- Review

- Personal concerns and prayer concerns

- Closing prayers

Daily walk

Bible readings

Day 1
Matthew 25:21

Day 2
1 Corinthians 12:22,25

Day 3
Ecclesiastes 4:9-12

Day 4
Romans 12:1-8

Day 5
Matthew 25:29

Day 6
1 Corinthians 12:1-6

Day 7
Ephesians 4:11-13

Verse for the journey

"Like good stewards of the manifold grace of God, serve one another with whatever gift each of you has received" (1 Peter 4:10).

Thought for the journey

When we use our gifts as God has intended, we become faithful in our common call to be an interdependent people. What do you think about this statement? How can you use your God-given gifts this week to become a blessing to those around you?

Prayer for the journey

Dear Lord, help me become appreciative of my gifts and talents and my responsibilities in their use. Never allow me to disgrace your blessings by giving way to selfishness and indifference. Amen

5 Challenged to Appreciate

Focus

Though we thrive on approval, the very thought that we are accepted for who we are and what we can do frees us to seek the higher ground of service to others in community.

Community building

Option

Affirm the tangible blessings of the person next to you by completing this sentence: "You, (*name*), can be thankful for _____."
(For example, "You, Gary, can be thankful for your beautiful art work in photography.")

Then, affirm the intangible blessings of the person next to you by completing this sentence: "(*Name*), I really like _____."
(For example, "Susan, I really like your smile. You cheer me up!")

■ Assign a number from 1 to 10 for each statement, 1 meaning "not true at all" and 10 meaning "absolutely the truth." Explain the reason for your choice.

Saying "I appreciate you" to someone (parent, spouse, sibling, colleague, or neighbor) is difficult for me because:

   a. the other person might think I have an ulterior motive. _____
   b. the other person might become very emotional. _____
   c. the other person might laugh at me. _____
   d. the other person might believe I am not telling the truth. _____
   e. the other person might feel I am insincere. _____
   f. the other person might not like it. _____
   g. the other person might say, "It's about time!" _____

Check-in

■ Share the results of the "Gift Cards" exercise from the previous session.

■ Offer suggestions for further action toward reconciliation.

> **Opening prayer**
>
> O God, you have given me so much in life. Grant me one more thing: a grateful heart for the people around me. Amen

Discovery

Romans 16:3-16

Read aloud and discuss the questions that follow.

3 Greet Prisca and Aquila, who work with me in Christ Jesus, 4 and who risked their necks for my life, to whom not only I give thanks, but also all the churches of the Gentiles. 5 Greet also the church in their house. Greet my beloved Epaenetus, who was the first convert in Asia for Christ. 6 Greet Mary, who has worked very hard among you. 7 Greet Andronicus and Junia, my relatives who were in prison with me; they are prominent among the apostles, and they were in Christ before I was. 8 Greet Ampliatus, my beloved in the Lord. 9 Greet Urbanus, our coworker in Christ, and my beloved Stachys. 10 Greet Apelles, who is approved in Christ. Greet those who belong to the family of Aristobulus. 11 Greet my relative Herodion. Greet those in the Lord who belong to the family of Narcissus. 12 Greet those workers in the Lord, Tryphaena and Tryphosa. Greet the beloved Persis, who has worked hard in the Lord. 13 Greet Rufus, chosen in the Lord; and greet his mother—a mother to me also. 14 Greet Asyncritus, Phlegon, Hermes, Patrobas, Hermas, and the brothers and sisters who are with them. 15 Greet Philologus, Julia, Nereus and his sister, and Olympas, and all the saints who are with them. 16 Greet one another with a holy kiss. All the churches of Christ greet you.

Praise and affirmation of one another is a basic cohesive factor in all healthy relationships. People who like and continue to appreciate one another with words of affirmation create a stable and delightful environment in which to coexist and make their relationship satisfying. We all need to be talked to, held close, and praised often in order to grow and mature in our own sense of self-esteem and appreciation of others. The apostle Paul demonstrates that people need praise and recognition. Notice that Paul had something good to say about many, both well-known and unknown in the community.

- Do we accept, affirm, and appreciate the contribution of women in our community?
- Who are the unsung heroes among us we have forgotten to recognize and appreciate?
- What can we do to express our thanks in order to draw them closer to us?
- What might be a modern equivalent to the ancient "holy kiss" as a gesture of acknowledgment?
- How would a community act, feel, and look if it engaged primarily in dissension?
- What is the connection between peace and praise?

A further look

Ask each group member to complete this exercise. Then, discuss the questions.

Check whether the following statements are true for your work environment or the last work environment of which you were a part.

Situation	Always	Often	Sometimes	Never
The boss/supervisor expresses displeasure at will.				
Employees' efforts are recognized.				
Job satisfaction among the workers is a priority for the company.				
Sexual harassment is evident in the workplace.				
People are assigned tasks according to their skills.				
Favoritism is practiced in the office by management.				
The basic mood of the workplace is positive.				
It is very easy to find colleagues willing to do "double duty" in emergency situations.				

- Do you feel supported in your work environment? Why or why not?
- What can you do to improve your workplace?
- What can you do to appreciate the other people in your workplace?

Consider this

"Nothing improves a child's hearing like praise."
Jerry D. Twentier, *The Positive Power of Praising People* (Nashville: T. Nelson, 1994) as quoted in "Lutheran Brotherhood's Newsletter Nuggets" May/June 1996

- Did you get a lot of praise as a child? Why or why not?
- What kind of praise meant the most to you?

Discovery

Luke 17:11-19

Read aloud and discuss.

11 On the way to Jerusalem Jesus was going through the region between Samaria and Galilee. 12 As he entered a village, ten lepers approached him. Keeping their distance, 13 they called out, saying, "Jesus, Master, have mercy on us!" 14 When he saw them, he said to them, "Go and show yourselves to the priests." And as they went, they

were made clean. **15 Then one of them, when he saw that he was healed, turned back, praising God with a loud voice. 16 He prostrated himself at Jesus' feet and thanked him. And he was a Samaritan. 17 Then Jesus asked, "Were not ten made clean? But the other nine, where are they? 18 Was none of them found to return and give praise to God except this foreigner?" 19 Then he said to him, "Get up and go on your way; your faith has made you well."**

Interpersonal relationships can stall when we are unable to receive gifts or compliments from others. That happens when we cannot say those simple words, "thank you." The ability to give thanks brings us into a cycle of joyful expressions of gratitude that builds relationships. Luke tells the story of a foreigner, one who is technically beyond God's blessings, who receives full blessings for his "attitude of gratitude." Relationships are enhanced by simple acts of gratitude.

- In what situation are you unable to receive gifts and compliments?
- How does it feel to receive someone's gratitude?
- To whom do you owe thanks?
- Considering the current state of blessings in your family, community, and church, to whom should you express a word of gratitude?

Pull it together

Distribute three, 3- by 5-inch note cards (preferably in eye-catching colors) to each person in the group.

- Think of at least one person to whom you can express appreciation and thanks this week.
    a. Think of a three-word message for your appreciation recipient. (For example, "You are terrific!" or, "Thanks for helping," or, "You're number one!" or, "Great job, Joe!")
    b. Write one of the three words on each of the note cards.
    c. Mail each card consecutively, a day apart, so that the recipient will receive a progressive appreciation message that week.

Wrap-up

Before you go, take time for the following:

- **Group ministry task**

- **Review**

- **Personal concerns and prayer concerns**

- **Closing prayers**

Daily walk

Bible readings

Day 1
Hebrews 10:24-25

Day 2
John 13:34

Day 3
Acts 2:42-47

Day 4
1 Corinthians 12:12-26

Day 5
Psalm 149:1-9

Day 6
Philippians 2:3

Day 7
Romans 12:10

Verse for the journey

"And the king will answer them, 'Truly I tell you, just as you did it to one of the least of these who are members of my family, you did it to me'" (Matthew 25:40).

Thought for the journey

Taking every opportunity to speak and act affectionately in appreciation is a basic component in all healthy and happy relationships. What do you think about this statement? How can you encourage someone with uplifting words and deeds this week?

Prayer for the journey

Holy God, from the beginning you have shown us your sacrificial love. Teach us to love sacrificially that we all may be one. Amen

6 Challenged to Commit

Focus

Harmony within the body is achieved when we receive and model God's committed long-suffering love for us.

Community building

Option
Write a definition of loyalty and share it with the group.

- As you consider your relationship with the following significant people in your life, what emotions well up within you? Use the following descriptions to help organize your thoughts:

abused	bored	anxious	depressed
restless	mad	happy	abandoned
laugh	encouraged	afraid	wanting to cry
disappointed	love	thankful	shout for joy
supported	used		

Relationships with:
a. your siblings
b. your parents
c. your children
d. your coworkers
e. your partner
f. your friends
g. your church family

- Share your feelings in two of the seven relationships.

Check-in

- Share the results of your "Three Word Message" exercise from the previous session.
- Offer suggestions for further action toward reconciliation.

Opening prayer

Help us to remember, O God, that there is no friendship without loyalty, no love without sacrifice, and no intimacy without commitment. Amen

Discovery

1 Corinthians 13:4-8a

Read aloud and discuss.

4 Love is patient; love is kind; love is not envious or boastful or arrogant 5 or rude. It does not insist on its own way; it is not irritable or resentful; 6 it does not rejoice in wrongdoing, but rejoices in the truth. 7 It bears all things, believes all things, hopes all things, endures all things. 8 Love never ends.

Human relationships must be governed by love because love will not allow us to harm another person. As believers in Jesus Christ, we are able to give love simply because we have experienced God's love. Love allows us to overcome the downside of any relationship and so delve deeper into the meaning of love. Love enables us to be together in the midst of our differences. In 1 Corinthians 13, Paul reminds us that love is the highest virtue and it outlasts the gift of time. Love is imperishable and in it we can find the resolve to maintain and nurture any relationship.

- Is love a top priority in your relationships? Why or why not?
- How do you reveal love in practical ways in your relationships?
- Who in your life is really hard to love?
- Are you a difficult person to love? Explain.
- What can love do to help overcome differences? Make practical suggestions for the group.

A further look

Provide meditative background music for this exercise. Read the Prayer of St. Francis aloud and with feeling. Allow sufficient time for meditation, then reflect on the questions.

A prayer attributed to St. Francis

Lord, make us instruments of your peace.

- How can God use you today as an instrument to bring peace to the struggling relationships around you?

    **Where there is hatred, let us sow love;
    where there is injury, pardon;
    where there is discord, union;
    where there is doubt, faith;
    where there is despair, hope;
    where there is darkness, light;
    where there is sadness, joy.**

- Can you think of broken relationships that embody hatred, injury, discord, doubt, despair, darkness, and sadness?

- Offer a quiet prayer in your heart for these relationships.

    **Grant that we may not so much seek
    to be consoled as to console;
    to be understood as to understand;
    to be loved as to love.**

- How have you handled inequities in your life?

    **For it is in giving that we receive;
    it is in pardoning that we are pardoned; and
    it is in dying that we are born to eternal life.**

    From *Lutheran Book of Worship* (p. 48) copyright © 1978

- Is there anyone you have not forgiven?
- Is there anyone who is angry at you?

Fade out the background music and give the final instructions.

- Close your eyes, relax, and take a deep cleansing breath.
- Let us pray the Lord's Prayer together.
- Share what you have discovered about "the act of love" through this exercise.

Discuss as a group.

Consider this

"If the proof is in the pudding, then it's important that love be in the church. We can talk all we want, claim and promise, engage in clever hype, but if, when they come into our churches, people find pettiness, complaining, power-tripping, jealousy, backbiting, and all that sort of thing, then they simply won't believe that we are authentic followers of the Lord of love."

LectionAid vol. 6, no. 2, Year C, p. 30. Copyright © 1998 LectionAid. Used by permission.

- Have you ever stepped into a "community from hell" that is void of love and compassion? What was it like to be in its midst?

- Give suggestions as to how a community can disagree agreeably.

Discovery

Philippians 2:1-5

Read aloud and discuss.

1 If then there is any encouragement in Christ, any consolation from love, any sharing in the Spirit, any compassion and sympathy, 2 make my joy complete: be of the same mind, having the same love, being in full accord and of one mind. 3 Do nothing from selfish ambition or conceit, but in humility regard others as better than yourselves. 4 Let each of you look not to your own interests, but to the interests of others. 5 Let the same mind be in you that was in Christ Jesus.

The church at Philippi was composed of people of diverse backgrounds, different lifestyles, and disparate social classes. The desire to be connected lies in a common faith and a common purpose for existence. The principle of like-mindedness is vital to any relationship, and people need to be committed to each other in humble accord. Paul speaks of personal and corporate humility, which fosters harmony in the home, community, or church body.

- What is the common purpose and goal of your relationships at home, the workplace, church, or in the community?

- What is the strength of your unity at home, the workplace, church, or in the community? Can you give examples?

- How will you resolve to console from love, share in the Spirit, and feel with compassion?

- What must you do to be committed to relationships at home, the workplace, church, or in the community?

A further look

Ask a volunteer to read John 18:1-11. Then read the story and answer the questions.

Aldrich Ames is among the most infamous double agents of our era. He is serving a life sentence in a maximum security prison. He worked for the United States Central Intelligence Agency for more than thirty years, and for a long period of time he was also an agent for the Soviet Union (and later, Russia), selling U.S. state secrets to its adversaries. In that disloyal exchange, Ames exposed more than one hundred intelligence operations, resulting in the arrest and execution of many U.S. spies to the Soviet Union. No one seemed to suspect him, even though he paid cash for a $500,000 home and the artwork it contained. It was a carelessly discarded document that exposed his divided loyalty.

- What causes a person to be disloyal in a relationship?

- What are the fallouts of dishonesty and deceit in a relationship?

- Does loyalty have its limits? Explain.

- How does the world view betrayal in a relationship? Contrast this with the teaching of the Bible (review John 18:1-11).

Individualism vs. community

Read and discuss the questions that follow.

Today we are caught in a cross fire of contradictory life principles and beliefs. Our quest to respect diversity in cultures, lifestyles, and religions has many people adopting a "do your own thing" attitude toward life. In light of such an attitude, we need to be courageous in our commitment to each other and, if necessary, even be willing to die for such commitment.

- Is it feasible today to speak of a "till death do us part" relationship? Why or why not?
- What does commitment mean to you?
- To whom are you willing to be committed and what are the benefits of such a commitment?

Pull it together

Discuss as a group.

- What did you learn about yourself in this chapter?
- Was this a difficult chapter? Explain.
- What is one thing you can do for yourself this week in light of this chapter?
- What is one thing the group can do for you this week in light of this chapter?
- Name two apprehensions you have in light of this chapter for your journey into the future?
- Join hands in a circle and pray a short prayer for the person on your left.

Wrap-up

Before you go, take time for the following:

- Group ministry task

- Review

- Personal concerns and prayer concerns

- Closing prayers

Daily walk

Bible readings

Day 1
Galatians 6:9

Day 2
Luke 14:26-28

Day 3
Proverbs 5:18-19

Day 4
Hebrews 13:4

Day 5
1 Corinthians 13:1-13

Day 6
2 Timothy 4:7-8

Day 7
2 Corinthians 8:10-11

Verse for the journey

"Where you go, I will go; Where you lodge, I will lodge; your people shall be my people, and your God my God" (Ruth 1:16).

Thought for the journey

When commitment is present, a relationship is secure and strong. When commitment is absent, we live with vulnerability and fear. What do you think of this statement? What practical steps can you take this week to ensure a loving commitment in your relationships?

Prayer for the journey

Lord, make us instruments of your peace.
  Where there is hatred, let us sow love;
  where there is injury, pardon;
  where there is discord, union;
  where there is doubt, faith;
  where there is despair, hope;
  where there is darkness, light;
  where there is sadness, joy.
For your mercy and truth's sake. Amen

Adapted from "A Prayer Attributed to St. Francis," *Lutheran Book of Worship* (p. 48) copyright © 1978

Appendix

Group directory

Record information about group members here.

| Names | Addresses | Phone numbers |

Group commitments

Do not be conformed to this world, but be transformed by the renewing of your minds, so that you may discern what is the will of God—what is good and acceptable and perfect. Romans 12:2

- For our time together, we have made the following commitments to each other

- Goals for our study of this topic are

- Our group ministry task is

- My personal action plan is

Prayer requests

Prayers

■ Closing Prayer

Lord God, you have called your servants to ventures of which we cannot see the ending, by paths as yet untrodden, through perils unknown. Give us faith to go out with good courage, not knowing where we go, but only that your hand is leading us and your love supporting us; through Jesus Christ our Lord. Amen

From *Lutheran Book of Worship* (p. 153) copyright © 1978.

■ The Lord's Prayer

(If you plan to pray the Lord's Prayer, record the version your group uses in the next column.)

Resources

DeYoung, Curtiss P. *Coming Together: The Bible's Message in an Age of Diversity*. Valley Forge, Pa.: Judson Press, 1995.

Flynn, Leslie B. *19 Gifts of the Spirit*. Wheaton, Ill.: Victor Books, 1994.

Harbaugh, Gary L. *God's Gifted People: Discovering Your Personality as a Gift*, expanded ed. Minneapolis: Augsburg, 1990.

Law, Eric H. F. *The Wolf Shall Dwell with the Lamb: A Spirituality for Leadership in a Multicultural Community*. St.Louis: Chalice Press, 1993.

Leas, Speed B. *Discover Your Conflict Management Style*. Bethesda, Md.: The Alban Institute, 1997.

Ortiz, Manuel. *One New People: Models for Developing a Multi-Ethnic Church*. Downers Grove, Ill.: InterVarsity Press, 1996.

Rhodes, Stephen A. *Where the Nations Meet: The Church in a Multicultural World*. Downers Grove, Ill.: InterVarsity Press, 1998.

Name _____

Address _____

Daytime telephone _____

Please check the INTERSECTIONS book you are evaluating.

- ☐ The Bible and Life
- ☐ Captive and Free
- ☐ Caring and Community
- ☐ Death and Grief
- ☐ Divorce
- ☐ Faith
- ☐ Following Jesus
- ☐ Integrity
- ☐ Jesus: Divine and Human
- ☐ Managing Stress
- ☐ Men and Women
- ☐ Parenting
- ☐ Peace
- ☐ Praying
- ☐ Reconcilable Differences
- ☐ Self-Esteem
- ☐ Smart Choices

Please tell us about your small group.

1. Our group had an average attendance of _____.

2. Our group was made up of
   ____ Young adults (19-25 years).
   ____ Adults (most between 25-45 years).
   ____ Adults (most between 45-60 years).
   ____ Adults (most between 60-75 years).
   ____ Adults (most 75 and over).
   ____ Adults (wide mix of ages).
   ____ Men (number) and ____ women (number).

3. Our group (answer as many as apply)
   ____ came together for the sole purpose of studying this INTERSECTIONS book.
   ____ has decided to study another INTERSECTIONS book.
   ____ is an ongoing Sunday school group.
   ____ met at a time other than Sunday morning.
   ____ had only one facilitator for this study.

-------------------- FOLD CARD IN HERE, SEAL WITH TAPE, AND MAIL TODAY! --------------------

Please tell us about your experience with INTERSECTIONS.

4. What I like best about my INTERSECTIONS experience is

5. Three things I want to see the same in future INTERSECTIONS books are

6. Three things I might change in future INTERSECTIONS books are

7. Topics I would like developed for new INTERSECTIONS books are

8. Our group had ____ sessions for the six chapters of this book.

9. Other comments I have about INTERSECTIONS are

Thank you for taking the time to fill out and return this questionnaire.

NO POSTAGE
NECESSARY
IF MAILED
IN THE
UNITED STATES

BUSINESS REPLY MAIL
FIRST-CLASS MAIL   PERMIT NO. 22120   MINNEAPOLIS, MN

POSTAGE WILL BE PAID BY ADDRESSEE

Augsburg Fortress
ATTN INTERSECTIONS TEAM
PO BOX 1209
MINNEAPOLIS MN 55440-8807

ST. ALBAN'S CHURCH
486 RATHGAR AVENUE
WINNIPEG, MANITOBA
R3L 1G3